Spiritual Hygiene

Sikander Malik

To my Mum and Dad

and Simrah

contents

introspection

if you ask who I am
I am nobody
in a black and white world of absolutisms
I dwell
in nothingness
belief systems
are only a false friend
I will wander alone
into the unknown

you belong to no person
you belong to no belief
you belong to no place
introduce yourself
to the wanderer
your soul wants to be

you can hear the symphony of existence
in aloneness

- solitude

aloneness and loneliness
are two different states

in loneliness you search for others
in aloneness you search for yourself

loneliness inside
comes from searching for companionship
within identities

begin
by seeking companionship
with your heart
and you will meet the universe
inside of you

our need to belong
is human in nature

true belonging
is found in the river of unconditional love

and absent in the security of labels

we have spent so long in our characters
that we have come to believe they are real
perhaps catching our reflection
for a fleeting moment
before we wrap ourselves up
in our blanket of security

you are the creation
you are the creator
you are the seasons
you are the oceans
you are the storm
you are the calm

these are your keys
to open the prison of a false
identity

if you have never
wandered into aloneness

you will remain a follower of ideas
that were never yours to begin with

this self
that you have come to believe in
is merely a collection of ideas

see them for what they are
and nothing more

often
the things we think we need
the most
are also what suffocate us
the most

if you have spent time
in your own being
the time you spend with others
will be sweeter

when we do not need to take
the soul yearns to give

protecting an identity
can give a feeling of security

something greater than security
lies within yourself

the poetic beauty in life
is found in ambiguity
don't be blindfolded with certainty

to experience life
bound by no identity
is to be like water
you may take the shape
of whatever your heart
desires

accepting
the limitations
of our belief systems
allows this life
to become an endless journey
of exploration

- the poetry of no belief

no matter how much you try and hold on
the evolution of life
will cause your old self to die
and a new one to form
true authenticity
is not holding on to the same beliefs
but to allow the natural evolution
of your mind and consciousness

to be truly alive
you must experience many deaths

I cannot *belong* to an ideology
you may know me
through the lens
of our inherently political eyes
but I cannot be separate
from you

- a universal truth

they tell you
you cannot just *be*
you must
sculpt
mold
and condition yourself
to be what they want you to be
I tell you
that you are already whole

if the words of deception
were packaged so beautifully
would they become your truth?
and if the words of freedom
were made so ugly
would they become your enemy?

in losing
your sense of self
you will truly find
who you are

the door
has always been open
but the prison
has always been safer
if you limit your mind to the self
you think you know who you are
if you expand your mind beyond yourself
you fall
into divine intelligence

I write for you
with a full heart
believing in the power of words
but they are just a seed
which can only grow from experience
I write for you
because I believe introspection
is more powerful than any scripture

the path beyond

I do not put a pronoun
beside god
as godliness is genderless

perhaps
the closest thing I had to God
was my own mother
this love was unconditional

consciousness
is not an organised truth
soak it in
taste it
feel it
but don't try to know it
just be here

I live
somewhere between
the confines of this world
and
my own being

my body and mind
belong to time
anything beyond that
is eternal

we were so focused
on the destination

we missed all the signs
on our journey

he called in the night
he called in the rain
he called in the sun
nothing came
until he realised
he was the darkness
he was the light
and there was nothing to come

we are
the children of the new world
entwining
with a newfound universality
we begin to lose a grip
on who we were

authentic love
is not for the sake of a creator
or promise of an afterlife
it is based in us
being individual manifestations
of a shared consciousness

- the truth of oneness

the preachers
are in business
and your soul
is a commodity

truth
belongs to no place
to no people
to no idea
truth is within you
and me

curiosity
with limits
is only an illusion
of freedom

most of the people around me
seem to be consumed
by things
that are not real to me

you have always been that which you are seeking

- wholeness

we are born
a blank canvas
as society
culture
religion
begin to paint our picture
the illusion
is so intricate
we forget
our canvas
was ever blank

breathe

hurtful thoughts
are judgments
of a past or future situation
they reflect
a *limited* view of self
letting go
of the attachment to the mind
reflects an *infinite* self

do not let
your mind
steal your presence

I can't entertain the fear inside
even when it grasps my neck
refusing to let go
I can't breathe life
into the thoughts
that make me not want to live
we are products of creation
but we are also creators
commit to thoughts
that create the conditions
for life to thrive inside of you
commit to shaping a new reality

fear only creates fear
acceptance
is your release

I am a friend of the present moment
a friend that often leaves
leaving me to bleed over the past
or yearn for the future
I must silence my thoughts
and find him again

it often feels
as though
there is a body
inside my own
it carries my fears
and traumas
it is reactive
in nature

in reality
it is a just a perception
perhaps a reflection
of the fearful mind

an illusion
that feels
so
real

sometimes
our demons are real
because
we made them real

this means we also have the power to
kill them

a hurtful thought
is a flicker of the candle flame
to become the thought
is to set fire to the entire room
it will burn out
in due time

be an observer

sadness
isolation
emptiness
you can sit here with me
I won't judge you
I am calm
I am present
I am breathing

in that moment
there was a kind of beauty
to my isolation
I had tasted life
both in bitterness
and sweetness

- dualities

a storm can cause chaos in the ocean
but once it passes
the ocean is left in serenity
if we learn to feel our emotions
without becoming them
the storm will always pass

life is seasonal in nature

if you have experienced the coldest of winters
the brightest summer days await you

to experience warmth
you must also know
what cold feels like

- lessons from dad

how many tears have you cried
for the child inside of you?

the only reality now is your present

but it is still ok to cry

- rebirth

the existence of suffering
is woven into the fabric of life
but you do not *always*
have to wear it on your sleeve

do not find an identity in suffering

in my being
is both light
and darkness

in moments of darkness
I lie
naked with my soul

shower the mind with grace
and the body
will soak up serenity

live
as though
you are already in the state of peace
your heart desires
and your reality
will change before your eyes

our thoughts become our reality

the me that I know
is a self
contaminated by perception
so how can I trust my thoughts?

your thoughts are truth
only if you allow them to be

cultivate the feeling of gratitude
view the world around you
with a childlike wonder
to *reunite* with a lost heart
and *separate* from a chaotic mind

in suffering
comes opportunity
to create
to refine
to *rise*

to create something
have the audacity
to believe in your ideas

don't worry
about whether what you want
is realistic

the consequences
of your so called idealism
are nothing
compared with the rewards
of your commitment
to shaping a new reality

- dreams

love

love
is the language of the soul
is the dialect of the universe
is never lost in translation
is never consumed by ego
is never stained with sin
is everything

you were bound by conventions
I just wanted to show you the other path
beyond beliefs
rules
appearances

- walk with me

relationships
are better left
experienced
not dissected

be wary of the destructive tendencies
of the analytical mind

in fear
you cannot let yourself fall

and it is beautiful to fall in love

feeding the ego
will leave you
constantly in a state of hunger

be vulnerable

forgive
because otherwise
you cannot be free

her heart was one of such sweetness
she was a pious Muslim amongst Muslims
a true Christian amongst Christians
an enlightened one amongst Buddhists
a flicker of light for sceptical minds
separation is created in the mind
unity is found in the heart

now you see
this was all just smoke and mirrors
obscuring the reflection
of our souls

she was a path
to my chosen destination
how could I allow anymore bitterness in my heart
when I carried her sweet heart in mine

a lover
is not yours to own
but you become one
in authentic love
uncovering areas of your soul
that would otherwise be left undiscovered

when I love her
I am loving
the universe
inside of a woman

our love is the pure white tablecloth

I hope the world doesn't leave a coffee stain
but if it does

I will spend a lifetime scrubbing

I am grateful
for your openness
to me

I know that I'm different
increasingly
unapologetically

in her presence
there is a stillness inside
she is the calm
in my storm

the seeds of enlightenment are scattered
throughout your soul

living through love and compassion

will lead to flowers blossoming
in the garden of your consciousness

as I change my perspective
the angels begin to sing to a different tune
the beauty of the world is a little more poignant
the smiles of strangers bring me bliss

- the mirror

often
the hardest part of loving someone
is letting go
the world can be cruel
but when we try to control things
we push away
what we were trying to preserve

I will go through my day
everyone will see me
but only you
will *see* me

- leaving my heart open

missing you
is a feeling
of wanting to be home

love
may I embody you
may you embrace me

even when fear tells you to be silent

do not

you are greater
than the sum of all my fears

ACKNOWLEDGEMENTS

This project would not exist without my parents being who they are.

Thank you to Leesya for the immense amount of love and support you give me.

A special thanks to Salma, Mahzabin and Nazma.

~

26768570R00072

Printed in Great Britain
by Amazon